jump the gun

jump the gun

poems

Jennie Malboeuf

AMERICAN POETS CONTINUUM SERIES NO. 213
BOA EDITIONS, LTD. * ROCHESTER, NY * 2025

Copyright © 2025 by Jennie Malboeuf

All rights reserved
Manufactured in the United States of America

First Edition
23 24 25 26 7 6 5 4 3 2 1

For information about permission to reuse any material from this book, please contact The Permissions Company at www.permissionscompany.com or e-mail permdude@gmail.com.

Publications by BOA Editions, Ltd.—a not-for-profit corporation under section 501 (c) (3) of the United States Internal Revenue Code—are made possible with funds from a variety of sources, including public funds from the Literature Program of the National Endowment for the Arts; the New York State Council on the Arts, a state agency; and the County of Monroe, NY. Private funding sources include the Max and Marian Farash Charitable Foundation; the Mary S. Mulligan Charitable Trust; the Rochester Area Community Foundation; the Ames Amzalak Memorial Trust in memory of Henry Ames, Semon Amzalak, and Dan Amzalak; the LGBT Fund of Greater Rochester; and contributions from many individuals nationwide. See Colophon on page 85 for special individual acknowledgments.

Cover Art: Ebsen Malboeuf
Cover Design: Sandy Knight
Interior Design and Composition: Isabella Madeira
BOA Logo: Mirko

BOA Editions books are available electronically through BookShare, an online distributor offering Large-Print, Braille, Multimedia Audio Book, and Dyslexic formats, as well as through e-readers that feature text to speech capabilities.

Cataloging-in-Publication Data is available from the Library of Congress.

BOA Editions, Ltd.
250 North Goodman Street, Suite 306
Rochester, NY 14607
www.boaeditions.org
A. Poulin, Jr., Founder (1938-1996)

for David, Mavis, & Eb

Contents

I.

Sex and Violence	13
Climate	14
Environment	16
Etymology of Gun	17
The Brass Bell	18
My Father Tells the Story of Seeing Tanya Tucker Dancing on a Bar	19
How to Drive in Snow	20
The Mirror of God Is Only Glass	21
Litany	22
Marigolds	23
Piety	24
New Town	25
The Part of My Father Will Be Played by Jack Nicholson	26
Every Time You Type *Moth*, You Type *Mother*	27
The Book of Eyes	28
In Vivo Paradox	29
Girl on Girl	30
Aging	31
Luster	32
Lakes of the Other Carolina	33
Year of the Bonfires	34
The Human Animal	35
The 20 Gauge is Meant for Birds and Beginners	36
animals making music	37
The Questionmark Butterfly	38
Invasion	39
Prophesy	40

II.

Hiatus	43
thaw	44
The Mass Shooter of the Day Lived on My Childhood Street	45
(another) Reinvention of the Beginning of the Universe	46
Prosperity	47
Algorithm	48
Land and Sky	50
As Soon as We Are Born We Start to Die	51
Appellation Before Christening	52
Stork	53
making a man	54
blonde boy	55
epiphany	56
Trigger Warning	57
Pentecost	58
Pastoral of the Upland South	59
Culling	60
Jeremiad	61
The Two Near-Deaths of My Father Like the Resurrection of *Roseanne*	63
Vanitas	64
The Position of the Sun in the Sky	65
Far Cry	66
Attrition	67
The Year We Met	68
No ideas but in objects	69
The Future	70
The Birth of the Moon	71

Notes	73
Acknowledgments	75
About the Author	77
Colophon	85

Blessed be the Lord, my rock, who trains my hands for war, and my fingers for battle.

Psalm 144:1

I.

Sex and Violence

               Blood   smells like metal, a p e n n y.
The contestants on gameshow reruns blasting

                  from the other room sound like murder victims
to me. Imagination outdoes reality. Brain w   a   v   e   s

can move a train. In 1988, the older girl next door
described the plot points of *A Nightmare on Elm Street*.

I cried so much I couldn't sleep for weeks.
She loaned me her leotard to wear home.

I was scolded for that, told not to run around in my underwear.
She once let me look up her shirt. Her body was years ahead.

These days, you detail a dirty movie you watched
and I'm jealous. Even snakes can tie themselves into a knot.

      We walked outside to a cop with an AR-15
this morning: a raccoon, rabid and loose.

I hurried the baby back in, the dog too.
You reminded me I'd seen this scene before.

                  A pit bull b l o o d i e d on the porch across
              from our old house. That a n i m a l should have
been   tamed.

Climate

Within months of us leaving the Carolinas, a house on the banks fell into
 the sea.
Five bedrooms now debris. Then, guns washed ashore after a suicide. But
 I still don't want
to be here.   This week you found out it cost

two-thousand dollars to take down a tree. The wind pushed so hard that
 even the stop
signs shook their heads. Even though we're a state away from reaching
 the ocean, water laps
against the windows at night. A wren caught himself in our screen door

in the early morning: his claws fingernail-like. I thought someone was
 breaking in.
When I was a kid, we used to clip my parakeet's nails. I accidentally cut
 them to the quick.
We'd let her fly and hit the ceiling, bathe her in the sink. A girl up the road
 would put her cat

in a pillowcase and swing it around. She'd howl and the cat would dart out
 in a zigzag after.
Since winter we can see the river sparkle from our bedroom. No curtains on
 the windows, no
leaves on the trees.   The church dome on the hill peeks out too.

I'm so tired of the pattern of snow then rain. Irony after irony, your
 suffering then mine handed
back and forth. Some day we'll say there was a time when we were all in
 love with our little family
when the dog was still alive when my hair had its color when the baby
 couldn't say words yet when

we wouldn't have traded it for any thing but sleep when we didn't worry
 about the windows, their
mouths agape. We've had sex in five of the eight rooms. Tonight a group of
 people

scratched the front door to see if this was a halfway house. We found
   antidepressants

with someone else's name when we moved in. You said you might buy a gun
   and not tell me
so we wouldn't hurt ourselves. I told my family not to give me one. I joked
   I'd blow my own head
off. We once saw a young girl wheel a propane tank down the street back
   home.

How stupid we were thinking she wanted to light a grill, have a cook out. By
   the final year we lived
there, makeshift kitchens popped up in other people's crawlspaces. The sea
   underground
made the limestone here.

Environment

The house is rotten. Lousy with bugs.
Yesterday springtails in the shower,
this morning a hum: in the bedroom window,
a wasps' nest. I didn't even notice until I overheard
someone next door stuffing our bin with other people's trash.
The lid won't close now, so when the garbage truck
finally brakes and squeaks down the street, I peek
               out and then into the comb's busy whirr.
Several dozen paper cells, little prisms packed with eggs.
I read in the newsfeed the only way we can save the planet
is to stop making more people. After that, we could stop
our travel, stop our tracks. I should be proud every
month when I see blood. Right after I lost my pregnancy,
I was told it was probably *for the best* because the baby
might not have *come out right*. A week or so back, we saw
a hornet's nest the size of a turkey in a tree.
I thought it was an owl at first. When I was a kid,
my dad cut down a two foot tall swelling, dropped it
in a black pillowcase,
                             shellacked and hung the whole thing
in a glass box that the Kmart threw away. He took the display
up to the school for everybody to see. These days he reminds
me how good I got it, hurries me to have children *before it's too late*.
The wasps in our window fashion their own paper from wood and spit-glue.
By autumn, they'll all die mostly anyhow. In the spring, the few queens left
will begin again.

Etymology of Gun

                    Someone handed me a gun and I hid it in a closet.
A millennium ago, a cannon was made to fit in a fist.
              Bamboo packed with powder in a hunt for immortality.
And then, in our time, a man—from a country Godless
                and cold that gave this easy weapon a name—shot
more people than any one on earth. The word *gun* means
            war not survival, is rooted in a feminine name that repeats:
war war like an echo, a ringing in the ear. In the armed forces,
      soldiers are told to name their rifles, to love them, own them.
The worst shooting in America for sixteen years was at the Luby's
      in Killeen, Texas. He hated women. One of his victims wanted
more guns after he felled both her parents and failed to end her.
        Man has always found a way to kill himself, turn a weed flower
into a gun instead of a crown. My mother first lived in a shotgun
        house: all the bedrooms on one side of the building, safely tucked
away. The story was you could get a clean line from one end
            to the other—front door to back—a bullet entering the home
without obstacle.

The Brass Bell

I rang it like I lived
in a happy home.
Like the white walls
shone with the Holy Ghost.
The old man from the t.v.
store gave it to me
when we bought a unit
wrapped in wood,
a piece of furniture
with flickering pictures
and bright lights. Inside
the store, a wall of glass
boxes all lit with the same
images. At home, ours
was broken; one reel ran
but the sound didn't carry.
We'd sit in front of it in awe,
little people *somewhere else*
I'd tell my brother
      without saying.
The new one stopped before
long. Its shell of a structure
took up three square feet
in the attic. Meanwhile
the brass bell, lime green
gnome atop, its crown, head,
shoulder, waist, mouth, lip,
tiny clapper. He is with me still.
Cheer, mirth. The Book of Daniel.

My Father Tells the Story of Seeing Tanya Tucker Dancing on a Bar

again. At a hotel lounge in western Kentucky, *she sang*
"Delta Dawn." He always says it like she was a wild woman.
It was the '80s. Her time. His too. He'd come home
in the middle of the night from a five day stretch coupling trains,
take us up to the corner diner while I was still in my nightgown.
He used to tell that story like a warning. The same way I couldn't
wear lipstick, hook my overalls on with purely one strap,
string my plastic rosary as a necklace. Now it's just a joke.

                                                      I imagine her boots,
leather pants, tight shirt hiding a bikini top you could only see if you cracked
open the record's centerfold. "Delta" wasn't even her song, it turns out.
But hers is the version everyone remembers. She was so young
when they put the track down she didn't know what *a cappella* meant:

                the story of man and *The Last Judgment* staining the walls. *And there*
she was, in the Time Out bar, no band had her back once more, heels on
the countertop, pedestaled, reaching for the rafters, working the cheap seats
with all she had. Before Michelangelo painted the ceiling
of the Sistine Chapel, he blotted out the fake sky and its stars.

How to Drive in Snow

Within a week of seeing
seven stars in the moon's
thick ring, it started to snow.

We are already weeks in,
snow deep in corners
and shade, refusing to leave.

At this point, it would be stupid
to call it quits. We finally drove
through town on what felt like

rails at the amusement park
last night—our own tin lizzy
machine. You sped round

the corner to *gain momentum*.
My mother said the worst winter
on record is still '77—the year

my brother was born. She drove
to the church in feet of ice just
to ensure a baptism, even

the priest scolded her.

The Mirror of God Is Only Glass

So the way it ends will be like the beginning,
the sun consuming the whole bound system it orders.
The most important star might turn into d u s t
        and that dust becomes new stars. The moon
will smack into Earth and dissolve into the oceans. At Fatima,
girls watched the sun spin and dance. My own father once
saw gold at the top of a hill and thought it to be God or Mary.
Mary, the mirror for us all: break its glass and bury it
deep. Like a Joseph statue for good luck—upside down
and six feet under. Enough of mirrors. They are water.
A watched pot my father mumbles, as I wait for a boy
to pick me up. The last time I hoped for beauty. The reflection
            with its own angles, a lit line of dancing dust.

Litany

Christ on the cross. Veronica
making a mirror from a rag.
There was a mouth of a river.
Fireworks too loud by the bridge.
Horse head on a stick for a pretend
pony doll. Cemetery where we rubbed
charcoal across paper to lift the names
off tombstones. Bologna with the red wax
ring. Donkeys at the state fair. Bench
with a vise like a holdfast. A bandsaw. Girl
with brown hair in a yellow yarn one piece
holding an electric drill on the wall of the garage.
A God's eye cross from popsicle sticks.
I had steady hands so I led the procession.
Chainlink fences with light green plastic privacy
strips. Four foot pools with fake wood walls clear-fell
from a pitchfork.   Communion
hosts cut from white bread with a bottle cap.
Police scanner, weather radio, wall clock
in every room, rifle under the bed, handgun
in the top drawer.
I'm older than God's child by now. I know the world
                        better than Jesus.

Marigolds

When I was fourteen my father chased two boys out
        of our house. They pushed the door open when I answered
it, walked all the way back to my brother's room,
            sat down to watch t.v. and play games. I could feel my father
    heading back down the street. Each step pumping blood
into my ears. I tried to get them to hurry up and leave,
          but they wouldn't. And when they finally listened,
   he crossed paths with them at the threshold.
       Marigolds are light-turning, they cry.
He asked me why they were in our house. And then,
    he made me get into our old station wagon and wander
           the alley streets until we found the boys again.
      They were once classmates of mine, one who I had a crush on
  for years—well into high school—and one who once asked me
    to take my clothes off when we were kids. It was an exchange,
      was how he explained it. This for that. But my father, heated
         and in the moment, jerked the car around to a drive
   near the church rectory. He hopped out, said things to them
that I couldn't hear. I refused to look. I kept
   my gaze on the priest's neatly trimmed yard. Little orange-yellow
flowers, little red-orange flowers decked with cream.

Piety

On the drive back from Richmond, after a wedding,
past the rundown strip club I drug you in
to cheer you up—where we barely watched the dancing girls,
just played pool in our church clothes—we stayed
in a motel 15 minutes past the state line. All we did was sleep.
I turned the lights on for a breath and quickly snapped the room black again.
When we woke, we stared at the brick red stain on the mattress,
the hole in the wall the size of a woman's head. One lamp didn't work,
your mother's funeral a bright young memory. We weren't ready
for so many things. Long before I knew you, I wore a mock sweater set
and tied my hair back the day I lost my virginity. I still fast two days
each spring, eat fish out of obligation.

New Town

We step off the curb into
glass diamonds. Confetti
cuts our feet; the drunks
mistake the street
for a trash bin and we crunch
more lotto tickets than leaves.
Where can we move to?
we take turns asking one
another. There isn't a night
lately that we don't hear *I don't
give a fuck* screamed two houses
down. And every neighbor
is old or killing themselves.
We've done our time you say.
Most often I agree—until
I catch glimpse of the fresh
white paint on the beadboard
of the porch ceiling.
Or I remember we stood still
and watched three foxes
wander softly from the schoolyard
a few weeks back.

The Part of My Father Will Be Played by Jack Nicholson

Big white teeth. My brother
reminds me *he isn't Irish*.
But the brows are the same.
Horned and intense, he'll do
a plum job.

In this scene, something isn't
right. The lighting is strange;
the furniture that was there
is now here. Or gone entirely.
Someone is standing in

the background that wasn't
just before. And that yawn sounds
like a door closing (or opening).
Everything looks normal but
one thing has blood on it.

I didn't mention the scariest
part   *jumpcut!*
a man in a bear suit.
You can't help but like him,
he commands attention

with broad arms or bright eyes
when seated. His face looks
crooked in the wrong direction
when you glance together in the mirror.

Every Time You Type *Moth*, You Type *Mother*

Inside the memory of the park
is the sandbox   with a shard
of glass that sliced your thumb: a ribbon
of blood pouring in a perfect spiral. Inside
the park is the concrete outbuilding crawling with
tent larvae. Inside the caterpillar is a poison: silk spun
and spit on everything it touches, a gauzy cobweb net
housed in the branches of fruit trees. Black cherry leaves kept
the pregnant mares fat the spring you made love the first time. That year,
the horses lost their foals by the thousands, some born still, some stopped
short of birth at all. It was a mystery at first. What the body does in a panic.
And so many dangers to come in the pasture. Pheasant's eye, milkweed,
snakeroot, bittersweet. Houndstongue, thorn-apple, gumweed, palm
of Christ. Even the ample goldenrod and dandelion are toxic. We don't
expect what tears us apart. Innocent kiss on the edge of a bed. A new horse
will stand within minutes of delivery; his hooves then his head slide out
in an opaque gray balloon. A different man will fill you 12 years later, almost
to the day. Trouble your womb, charge you with life. A neat line of nothing
at its hollow end. Blood from a stone.

The Book of Eyes

When I touch my lashes,
a reflex: mouth opens wide,
a dead-on ghost.

                The light
in the hall makes it too dim to see.
Daddy asks if I'm *lining* my eyes.

He means with navy eyeliner.
Halloweens used to be for
the makeup bag with the blue iris

against a white background.
Shadow, shadow. Novelty eyes.
Who are we when no one sees?

The face of God is water.
The eyes of the world are fire.
On the t.v. murder show,

they tell the story of a killer
who scooped the eyes from his victims,
mostly whores.   When found out,
it was never said why. He drew page
after page of eyes forever
and adorned the walls of his cell.

In Vivo Paradox

Cat in a box. As of right now,
the night before my ultrasound:
he is both alive and late. A glass
brimming with poison could spill
at any moment and I'd never know.
I was pulled from a scar on my mother's belly.
Before me there was another possible child.
The rabbit is always dead—whether her egg
stores swell with women's signals or stay unbothered.
My mother tells me now she's sure I ate squirrels
at some point. My father dispatched them in the early
morning hours in an even more rural past. In a dresser drawer
I kept a worn rabbit's foot. I imagined somewhere ruby eyes
that scared me. I wished for a different life, not knowing what it would be.

Girl on Girl

        she tried to kiss me once.
me, the cat's paw.
  we used to crowd the bar
     with   cotton skirts,
        perfect
                breasts, long stringy hair
     loose as corn silk;
    no beer cold enough to stay icy
  when it wet our warm mouths.
                cupped hands
to the other's ears, elbowed arms
knotted tight.
    it would hurt her to say
that I was happy.   feel
so now. saw most of those men
    we said we'd *die* for
        naked and joyful.   wanted to shake them,
     jerk some sense   get close enough to
    say *can't you see what she is?*
our eyes kept sidelong to make sure
         we were
being watched

Aging

On the day   before my birthday, I played s h a d o w
      with a crow. Each laugh of his,   I echoed back
  until he flew his perch. I thought I might win. Then   he returned
with two more crows on his   l i f t ,
staking his claim on the floodlights.

                    I thought I might pull him down
to my level.   He quieted, cocked his head.
                    He moves closer to God by nature,
  pushes a i r beneath him like years.

Luster

We baptized ourselves in the Atlantic
three weeks after your mother died.
After days on end of cheap beer, we dared

each other to skinny dip. The nightsky
so dark we fell into every depression
in the sand. You told me you'd never

marry; then we had sex on the hard silt.
I could scrape my teeth across your shoulder
and know you were the real deal. Other boys

were fool's gold. Nuggets of grit embedded
in my back. The dog puked on my party skirt
with the metallic embellishments

on the drive home. We pissed off our hosts:
out-laughing them, out-coupling them—a pillow
wedged behind the headboard, pulling

my dress down on the front porch. Our own bedroom
ceiling's drywall buckles and sparkles with pyrite.
The shingles' fiberglass worn by moonglow. These days,

I'd kill for a private beach like that one. Even though
it was never ours to begin with. Ghost crabs haunting us
just under the surface of sunlit glitter.

Lakes of the Other Carolina

                Little River, Dead River.
Man-made lake stocked with redear sunfish,
        perch, the improved bream, cherry gill, shellcracker.
    Alcohol and Drug Abuse Lake. Pepsi Cola Lake.
                Creek where we rowed a john boat into a mouth
treed with pines. Water where I called my mother
      high. Basement of a big lodge house where I wept
          and thought I was telling the truth.
      Motel where we waited to try for a baby, then watched
the moon black out the sun. Bows, crooks, arches sweeping
        the floor full-dress and clocklike. Horsepasture River.
Most of the world is saltwater, followed far away by ice.

Year of the Bonfires

We built one or two each week.
Then eventually every night.
Gathering twigs from the yard
at first. Sticks the size of whipping
switches. They burn high and quick.
They pop like gunpowder. After
the lot was clear, we searched the alley
where our neighbor watched
our other neighbors fuck for broken
tree limbs, hoisted them over the fence,
found perfect logs and you carried them
on end for sport. By the end of the year
we were pulling the shakes off the outbuilding,
breaking it down piece by piece, finally buying
firewood by the bag, the kind I joked
that Christmas smell is added to. We burned
the picnic table and chairs, cardboard boxes
and packing paper, nails and old dolls,
brush that was still a bit green.
The flames reached so high they kissed
the canopy of branches overhead.

The Human Animal

Charles Manson is Dead as the world loses order,
chokes itself in a pell-mell haze.
His mother sold him for a glass of beer.

His son killed himself. No wonder:
                the shame, his wild gaze.
Sharon Tate is dead and he gave the orders;
he invented God, who invented murder.
                His mother sold him for a glass of beer.

He named himself *Christ, a jug of wine, a boxcar*,
claimed there were *all kinds of Jesuses*.
Charles Manson is Dead as the world loses order—

presidents and kings, guns and borders.
His insides started bleeding, his mind a maze
with no safe exit. He handed out knives but couldn't
                be there.

That jagged third-eye tattoo gone if for a kind word.
Charles Manson is Dead as the world loses order.
His mother sold him for a glass of beer.

The 20 Gauge is Meant for Birds and Beginners

In our house, the birthday banner we use and reuse
all the special days has fallen off the wall—tape failing
on one side and stuck too high to remove on the other.
                                      A song gums inside my head.
I saw pictures of Kurt Cobain's waist and feet, a cop holding
his rifle. I had always envisioned a handgun, imagined
an empty room but not a greenhouse. The Christmas
of 7th grade, they were on t.v. all the time. Lilies around,
Neil Young said he sounded *like a werewolf.* Then that spring,
kids at school made easy jokes about his last name. *Ka-bang!*
                                  Each boy had their records.
The naked baby baited with money, someone's insides
on the outside. Everyone lays claim, an echochamber—
his widow says one song is about her vagina, "In Bloom"
might be the guy who gave him the gun. And the footage
of them holding their infant on heroin. I'm past his age,
my baby past his baby's age, my marriage past
his marriage's age. I don't even like
his music that much.

animals making music

goats and parakeets sound like men, men like God.
every sound the throat crafts a mimic. we try to teach the baby
about joyful noise, banging keys on the piano, tapping sticks
                                      on a makeshift bucket drum, bending
and plucking the strings of a tiny guitar. whales and birds sing, crickets play
their own legs, elephants trumpet, the baby copycats them.
the loud words in books he likes best. at two, he reads *boom* and *moo*
and *pop pop pop*. he giggles. relishes the fright. but his own hiccups keep him
awake. there's a yellow moth in China that makes like a bat to jump
his mate. he hums a whisper song
                    so she'll move in close, thinking she needs him, she's in danger.

The Questionmark Butterfly

While we blew bubbles that shine oil and water like carnival glass,
we caught glimpse of what looked to be a moth. A fake,

an impersonator for sure. With its wings closed, it posed
as tree bark. And then a blink opened orange and black.
Not quite a monarch's stained glass, the white rind of zest's pith

turned on its ear. This pattern gently speckled. The baby wanted to poke
him with a stick. I said *that will break him*. I said he's like *paper*.
History is recorded like the memory of a small child:
nothing at conception or even birth, then one awful something at two.

A tiny trauma, mother and the others leaving for Tennessee,
my wet hands pounding the screen door, grandfather yelling *shut up*.
Then nothing for years more. Until events squeeze tighter together
into a timeline. I worry what the baby will recall first about the world.
I know now what we saw wasn't a moth. That he wanted the nectarine

I cut first for the dog, then left for the birds. He might have been drawn
to something else entirely—carrion? What was once sweet
                                        but at present rotting.

Invasion

The first spring you came back home
your sister's dog whelps on the bedroom floor.
You hated the dog. Her breath, yellow teeth,
greasy hair, belly fat with pups. No one
was in the house. The dog coming open
and careworn. Her offspring: gummed and noncolors.
You reached your hand almost-inside to move
what's wedged behind her. And each immovable
problem heavies itself in a pile. Nine, ten, eleven, twelve.
A dozen lives kicking. The source dog labored and spent.

Prophesy

> *Desert animals will move into the ruined city, and the houses*
> *will be haunted by howling creatures. Owls will live among*
> *the ruins, and wild goats will go there to dance.*
> Isaiah 13:21

Three nights in a row, we watched a bird of prey watch us.
He was silent and cut our path twice. The third time
we thought we had missed him. But on our last turn,

there he was: perched on an old metal handrail, slow
pivot to make a near perfect circle of a stare. I tried not
to move. I took in his face to note its shape—the lack of heart,

a true owl. *An omen* we joked. Maybe death, maybe fertility.
When we got home I read Isaiah backwards. What is it that empties
each bedroom and fills it with beasts?
                            What angered the Almighty at that hour?

Once oxygen was present in the world, animals could commence.
In Genesis, God gifts Adam with a showing of animals. Here in the air,
there breathing in swallowed water, heavy on the ground.

At twilight, we teased and scared each other. *He's right behind you!*
one of us would cry out. I wanted to rush the end before it arrived,
jump the gun to call the big *surprise!*

II.

Hiatus

The day I lost another job offer to take us
home, I hear from a friend she's moving to Hawaii.
We spotted a stray killdeer by the riverbank that morning—
his odd striped neck a sure sign of a shorebird misplaced.
Hundreds of miles from the coast.   I can't seem to draw a bead
on what exactly I am missing.   When you were 13, you looked
for Halley's Comet in the sky. You told me you thought it'd be
brilliant and clear like a star. But it was *dull like a cotton ball*. Muted
and veiled. Blurry and lackluster.   You were *looking at the wrong thing*.
     Fourteen years ago, the core of the earth stopped and started spinning
  the other way. Maybe this moment is an opening.   Or a gaping mouth
that will swallow us whole.   Wind and water swell high around here. I wake
to lightning. Wait for the faraway clap, more frightening the longer it takes.
    The night they pulled our baby out of me, the blood rushed to my head.
                    I couldn't see anything, held my breath.
    And then a wail. Now when I hold his hand, we stare at our shadows
            on the sidewalk. Standing dead in front of us,
                   the sun behind. You said *divers can only go so deep*
               before the weight of water crushes their lungs.
               Air, like dreams, will give way to pressure.
Only animals
            like flashlight fish
                  can spend a lifetime at those depths.
     Mostly because they never rise
                        to the surface to begin with.

thaw

no one knows how to restart the world
it's not just me with
a lonely pregnancy and a lonelier motherhood

after the cold snap
we walked the dog and the baby
by the river
and saw two boys in their early
teens walking across the frozen water

they yelled up to us, joked around
i couldn't help but tell them to be careful

as we rounded the corner we heard one yelping
and later saw him walking home
with a frown and wet from head to toe
the birds move like swarms of bees now

almost every animal we see is vexed

those boys said they saw a fish still stuck in the ice
of the river branch—suspended, petrified
and on the way back a young mother

                                            with three toddlers let them play
                                                unwatched in the front yard

                                              she only surfaced from inside
                                    when the babies found a dead bird
                        covering his body with a white napkin, scolded
                              the lot of them for stirring up trouble

                        all the while our old dog paints the sidewalk
                          with a bloody paw, stops every two houses
                                                to take a rest

The Mass Shooter of the Day Lived on My Childhood Street

Just two turns, a left and a right. The name changes but the path from door
    to door moves like a snake. He was born in a state just to the north,
went to school in a state just to the south. He killed 5 people, almost 6,
        4 blocks away from where my grandmother died well into her 90s.
Two blocks east my brother started thinking
                      he should take a gun to work—
the threat of violence following him from his car to the lobby of his building.
    The city's fire hydrants the same color as orange hunting caps.
I trick-or-treated at his house before he ever thought of living there,
        before he was born. His nextdoor neighbor a little girl
two grades down now all grown up. Microphone in her face,
 on the 6 o'clock news, laughing nervously, saying *we thought he was square*,
that *we were the loud ones around here. Mental illness?* she guessed.
    In the tiny town we live in at the moment, a little boy with a BB gun practiced setting his sights on us while we walked with our baby and dog
 at the park. He'd march a few steps, stop and aim his rifle in our direction.

        My family promises to teach my child to one day shoot a gun.

(another) Reinvention of the Beginning of the Universe

Now they say asymmetry started it all.
Some static p o p in blackness, an imbalance
of mass and nonmass, energy there and not there.
        Each day more planets are found—a star with six earths
circling it. Many things unexplained.

I used to play a game and see what points in the room
I could move to and not show up. Where could I avoid being
seen in the mirror—it was like I didn't exist. I was a vampire.
At night I'd ask my mother to cover the glass with a sheet,
which made it worse, I suppose. The white linen hung against the frame
and hovered feet off the ground: a perfect ghost.

Prosperity

              At the top of the hill,
streets trimmed with marigold and lunaria,
sat the little church, where every year

my mother worked the Big Six booth,
money laid flat on lucky 32, leather strap
slapping each spoke of a fortune wheel:

the board raised, dimes slid into a strongbox.
The men drank in the beer garden after
frying chicken and fish all day. Milk and honey

like so many silver dollars and gold.
My grandmother tossed her pull-tabs
in the parking lot, and later on, she rode

the gambling boat up and down the Ohio.
The chances bought into like seed faith.

Algorithm

People like you liked this home.
People that work at the post office or a school.
People that wake at 5:32 to drive to somewhere high and dark
to see the p l a n e t s a l i g n e d above the crescent moon.
People whose fathers unloaded meat trucks when they were laid off
from the railroad in 1983. People whose fathers never came home.
People who saw a deer in an abandoned parking lot for the nearby mill.
People who have wished death on most other people. People
    who have wished
        death for themselves. People who choose
                a city based on how long the drive
                    will be to their hometown. People who feel
    like they have no future.
    People who let their yards get overgrown   with apple trees and ivy.
            People who forget
      to rake until the next summer—the lot opaque
            with mosquitoes and lit by fireflies.
People whose mothers died suddenly. People who already mourn their living
mother's death. People whose dog bit a friend. People who've been told
they're too loud. People who've been told they're too quiet. People who
still have baby teeth in their thirties. People who are prematurely
    gray. People who buy each other rotary telephones for Christmas.
People who try to make their new house look like all the old houses
        they've lived in. People who have had miscarriages
and no children. People who rarely fight. People who bruise
their hands against the counter when they do. People who have good sex.
    People whose accents
come and go. People who like the color green. People who spend
one hundred dollars a month on birdseed. People whose mulberries
were ravaged by waxwings. People whose windows
get nested by wrens.   People whose brothers and fathers hunted
        rabbits. People who don't want
to own a gun. People who dream their spouses must be leaving soon.
People whose spouses tell them *that's silly*. People who are unsure
of some things that happened to them. People who like bungalows.
Five acres. A house built before their parents were born.

People who watch too much
television. People who've found live snakes inside their homes.
People who hiss
at their neighbors' dogs to stop them from barking. People that can play
any stringed instrument. People who can
almost sing. People who took an ax to a hope chest.
People who want to know where they belong.

Land and Sky

This year the Northern Lights could be seen
from Indiana. The sun painted the night
with a neon aurora.   Once,
my father drove us across the river to see
about a house. It was surrounded by nothing.
Tree-less acres and wet ground. I peeked in
and could see   down a long hall.

The room I planned for myself on the ride back
would be quiet—a quilt on the bed, a birdcage
in the corner. My father has lived at the same address
since before he could walk. When he wanted to marry
my mother, they were so young the Church asked
their parents for permission. Soon after, they kept
a fat mutt in the backyard and paid cash to make it

all belong to them. Each year, the dog whelped
a new litter and, later on, one of their children shot
starlings from a cracked window in the kitchen.

As Soon as We Are Born We Start to Die

You said your childhood home
was *emptied out* and I pictured
a giant hand picking the house up
and shaking about its contents,
little startled people and all.
My favorite part of playing dolls
used to be dressing the rooms; choosing
a place for each piece of furniture:
the tiny computer with squiggly lines,
a *ringaling* wind-up phone, plastic
couches and paper rugs, a petting zoo
of felted flocked foxes out back.
By the time I'd get to putting on
the girl-dolls' clothes and shoes,
dinner was on the table.

Appellation Before Christening

Deemed worthy of a child.
Every so often, I think of it:
first baby, what could have been.
Granted, I didn't know
how an infant would fit
in our new marriage;
just six weeks in, we joked.
Kicks? Your large hand
laid across
                        my belly.
No way, I pushed free.
On a lark, we tore open a box, I
pissed on a magic stick,
quietly panicking while a blue cross
rose to the surface.
Such disbelief, your mouth open,
tears baptizing my face.
Undone within two weeks time.
Violently sleepy, dog-tired, and ill,
we watched a still yolk sac be
examined on a static screen.
Years have turned to ghosts, entire
zoos repopulated.

Stork

    Three times you crowded my doorstep.
            A blanket with troubles inside.
A coverlet shaded some changed color.
Painted black and white, you are far
from such clarity.
            I moved back home,
away from deep waters. I rearranged the stones
outside, washed the green off my house.
Your own babies sound like cats and snakes.
You yourself knock like a gun. And you're a hypocrite
like the rest of us: killing your own young
to save yourself. You preen but your feathers are still
thick with lice. On the nape of my son's neck you left a scar.
What did I do wrong? I parried your visits for years.
We enjoyed making babies

                            too much. You toss your head
                back as a threat, just to say hello.

making a man

to the baby, every new shape of a creature reads precious.
every dog called by our dog's name. the most giant beasts
become *elf-ants*. when he imitates an owl it's as if he is crying.
before we visit the zoo for the first time, we watch a cat
i chase off the porch. the baby smiles, begs to pet her.
the cat hisses. last night i heard her calling in heat.
i learned these lessons long ago. animals can be brutal,
nature can be cruel. our old dog snaps at my husband
when he helps her onto the couch. i used to pick up books
in my apartment and silverfish would dart out from underneath.
i went to the beach alone and came home with swimmer's itch.
						a whale's heart is as big as a man.
							of all the birds, owls see blue.

blonde boy

will your hair stay so white?
your father's turned dark then gray.
first the edges of his temples peppered
then his whole head covered in dust. his beard
hiding his adam's apple. we watch you try
to eat rocks, the foundation of the house.
alongside, our old dog tries to eat her own body.
we had hoped for a daughter:
her wide eyes and pin curls, learning
about planets and birds. a universe i could open
to her that was a locked house for me.
a zenith or a heron's nest.
but this world has always been yours.
throwing and hitting, we know now already
what you will be, could become.
a boy's boy, a man's man.
how do i raise another
in a line of so many who have done such harm?
i look at your face and see my father,
i look at your face and see my own.

epiphany

my baby wants to turn me into a bird.
he points to my nose and then his toy owl
and says *beak beak*. i make my arms into wings.
fly he says and signals upward. he watches me sing.
i sing only for him. i have a body of air. glide and lift.
see my hands disappear, my skin sprout downy feathers.
soon i will pluck feathers with this nose-mouth from my own
breast to build us a nest. at first, when he'd call me *mama*
he struck my chest. i thought he was looking for m i l k
but it was the ribcage inside he named. a sternum,
an axis that would permit me   to wheel and r i s e .

Trigger Warning

I couldn't remember what the paper was called:
onionskin? a friend suggested. *Thin skin*,
we laughed.
                              Just the term
before, a group of students wanted an opaque
page in front of any troubling words.
What kindness: to warn the one you plan
to kill. Every hurt has a curtain; sheer layer
after layer of see-through unfurl
until the hard core is exposed.
Who floated this idea?
The first aircrafts were   k i t e s. Delicate
and fragile. Heavier-than-air.
The wind carried them along a beach scene, set them off
at nothing. A safer image traced to a second sheet.
Our own skin is no protection.
Slights pierce like light through water,
                    any little bullet
          a meteorite
                    exploding
                              our sky.

Pentecost

The dentist wants to cut my tongue.
Several times he says I lisp a little.
Say sixty-six? he asks. I try my best
to sound adult. Under my baby tooth
still hides a fang. At 15, a cavity
ate through my molar. I used a fine-tipped
tweezer to pick away bits of food, clean it out.
It was weeks before I told my mother, months
still before we could pay for a root canal.
At night, I grit my jaw until my smile
becomes a perfect bite, and my bone pops as
I part my lips. I look down at a handful
of ivory, tongue at bloody gums.
        On White Sunday, the priest
wears red.   In my book of Sacraments, mote
flames hovered above the men's brows and crowns.
Eve was the first to speak, not name, and she spoke
            to an animal with a fork in its head.
My tongue lies on the floor of my mouth.

Pastoral of the Upland South

My mind spins a yarn to scare itself.
We thought we were rid of
the piles of brush and then,
sitting there for days, they found us.
Man knocking at the door. Brush with
a brown snake inside. We had to carry it all
down the access road again. Break it
into smaller sticks, tie it tightly with twine
and strings from the kitchen, legs eaten
by mosquitoes, cuts on our arms,
bits of shingles and drywall littering
the grass like bomb shrapnel. Just
the day before, my mother called
to say *it has rained so hard here*
the blooms are blowing off the flowers.
That night we woke to a tick
crawling up my hand.

Culling

The neighbors behind us built a coop.
Hammering for weeks, then a rooster crowing
all hours of the day. The brood teased our dog,
got her digging at the fenceline again. I stood
as close as I could get and cackled. Tried
to rile them. Then, just yesterday, we watched
the man of the house hold the biggest chicken
by his talons and carry him upside-down
to a white table, grab a maddock, press a knee
over a wing, and swing until his head flew into
the air. Both of us were dumbstruck. The back gate
itches with orange trumpet flowers.

Jeremiad

> *Woe unto them that join house to house, that lay field to field,*
> *till there be no place, that they may be placed alone in the midst*
> *of the earth!*
> Isaiah 5:8

My husband has already started packing our things.
I spent the day yelling shut up behind a closed front door
to the street like a coward.

I slept late into the afternoon, dreamt of strolling into houses
that were taken, a whole town of bungalows for us to spy on.
We really did that once—walked into the wrong house looking for

a friend in the suburbs. The occupant didn't see or hear us and kept
chopping vegetables, back turned. We could've been stabbed. What did
the two of us know about order. His two-story childhood farmhouse
    caving in,

billboards, apartments, duplexes leaning on the eaves. The home I grew up
    in protected by
chainlink fences. My father could name everyone around us: the only place
he's ever known. The police, the promise of violence, our car kicked in,
    the racing stripes

down our Ford Escort never straight again. For the third time in a matter
    of months,
a gun's gone off while my husband was at work. Two drive-bys, one
    accidental discharge.
We hit the floor of our living room when across the way a do-nothing fired
    his pistol

into the sky.   These days, on either side,
single men that look like serial killers. A half a block away, a man knifed to
    death.
In the hours that followed, the neighbors picked through his belongings,
    thanked God for the new

dining room table left by the curb.   We saw another man beat the shit
    out of his girlfriend.
On the front porch. Push her down, knock her teeth out. Her mouth bloody
    and weeping a shroud
bib on her Easter dress. On Mother's Day, someone next door ate our trash.
    I came from

a state with nothing but caves underground, fault lines, rivers and lakes.
    There is nowhere
to go. Nowhere to turn back toward. The lone person nearby we talk to,
    we've called
the cops on several times.   Daddy once threatened to shoot our neighbor.
    Last night,

we heard an alley cat scream on our porch—said it must be mating season
    again but woke
this morning to a snake with one pierced hole straight through his head.
    The same one scooted off
to the bushes the day before. My father hired three ex-cons to build a fence
    along his back lot.

Concrete, metal. Two men high.

The Two Near-Deaths of My Father
Like the Resurrection of *Roseanne*

Inside the t.v., my childhood.
Always the talk about unions,
always the talk about class.
The father in father clothes.
The mother in mother hair.
Both daughters me. The couch
orange and brown with an Afghan
blanket draped across its back
like a flag. On the kitchen table,
plastic bottles of ketchup and dressing,
cans of RC cola and beer, meatloaf
and mashed potatoes. Our Kmart sheets
and quilts on the beds. A rotating cast
of next-door neighbors. Aunt letting
herself in the back door. On the last episode,
Daddy dies of a heart attack. Then, he's brought
back to life. On the last episode, the show's star
goes in for knee surgery and the series ends.
The family starts to unravel, five months after
the daughter's marriage, three months after
miscarriage. [Railroader] father. The [one true
Church. Housewife] mother. A little family
that no longer exists. The last of the nuclear
Americans: [Jesus, Mary, and JFK on] plates
across the kitchen walls. [A metal barn
thermometer in the entrance to the hall.]
A [pink] room whose color is never
replaced. Something tragic,
    someone laughing
loudly as the screen
goes black.

Vanitas

Six years and one month in
and your bouquet of flowers dries
out on the kitchen table. Every time
I think of babies I think of death.
By the time we raise just one,
the hourglass bottom-heavy, our youth
becomes the empty air. Your teeth
are longer each year—you feign surprise
at the gray trimmings on the floor
around your barber's chair. My complexion
folds; I feel my skull poke from under
my fat cheeks. What is it that we want to raise?
Another future skeleton. A waste of time.

The Position of the Sun in the Sky

Just as we realize we might want
children, the world slows to a crawl.
You brought a butterknife to bed, a mirror
to the kitchen. I woke up talking about tulips
after my d&c. Even in the twilight room, I was trying
to be pleasing. The body still thinks
it's pregnant after miscarriage. Not until
weeks later does its hair thin, its skin freckle
with blemishes. The body knows it's a mother
in its bones: the pelvis hit by birdshot to a coroner.
Everything moves so easy these days. *Analemmata*:
an S in the sky completes to an 8.

Far Cry

In the shower I made song with my throat and a soapy wand
with my forearms. It swelled illusion on my belly.

Magic. A bubble. An accident at first, then I couldn't let it go—
or hold that position forever. The mother whale

who carried her dead baby for 17 days will birth another
calf. Her first she pushed for 1000 miles.

                                        Seventeen days like 17 months.
I held onto you for seven like a teddy bear, proof I tried to be

a mother.   (I don't know what I want. I have decided not to try again.)
Whales sing to find other whales. Like dogs who are lost.

They listen for a soft answer, an e c h o in the distance.
This morning two blue lines rose to the surface: one dark and loud

as midnight, the second almost fading away.   (I am not who I thought
I would be.)

Attrition

                        You took
those naked pictures of yourself to share
with someone special. Every once in a while
you find your mind worrying over it—
thinking you should have blackbarred
your eyes, pixelated your face rather,
just taken them from the neck down,
or not at all.
That strange man
so excited when he received them
called you straight away   breathing
h e a v y in your ear
promised a year later he *wouldn't show a soul.*
Those unknown hangups for a year after that.
But your hair is so different now,
your mother's pink and blue flowery curtains
from the background in a box
tucked deep.

The Year We Met

I am your mother dying.
My face is eighteen empty bottles
lined up along your kitchen counter.
A wet finger circling the lip, a makeshift glass harp,
       a mouth half-covering a jug like a pipe.
          My singing voice her ashes, my arms full with
              a heavy box of empty jars she saved.
The house in shambles, abandoned cars rusting in the front yard,
the phone number cut off. I am the horse she jockeyed
where her father lived downstairs and raised another family.
Her dog shot at the end of the access road.

In your new town, I am no running water, no heat, a one story
starter that turned into your only home. I am the tattoo
of your father's name before he left her.

No ideas but in objects

Home from our wedding,
we found the oldest picture
of you with your mother
soaked in bourbon
on the backseat of our car.
Audubon's sketches were eaten
by rats. A mischief of kittens nesting
in his life's work: thousands
of renderings of rare Southern birds.
Your mother gone years already,
birds migrating to another continent
for the winter.
                              You told me once
that if something ever happened
to me, you'd never marry again.
Your needs could be met
by prostitutes. Sweet nothings.
All of those animals, their likenesses,
were drawn again, but better.

The Future

> *...animals mark the sea changes in our lives.*
> Miller Williams

Five years ago this season, we took
the dog to the beach for the first time.
Our marriage in its infancy, she was still
      young then, afraid of the giant
bathtub that was the ocean. We never let
her off the long leash, for fear she might get
swept away. That night, all three of us slept hard
in a sandy king-sized bed in some dirty motel facing the water.

The Birth of the Moon

What hit you has become you.
Pieces of the bullet embedded
in your skin. Even
that which you come from
will never be the same.
But from violence comes
the tides, the seasons.
Your movement a timepiece.
Your surface a veil of dust:
on a bright face,
water turns to stone.

Notes

The book's epigraph is taken from Psalm 144 in the *New American Standard Bible*.

The author would like to acknowledge the prior existence of Jaimee Hills' poem "Tonight the Character of Death Will Be Played by Brad Pitt."

"The Book of Eyes" references the story of Charles Albright, a convicted serial killer in Texas.

"Prophesy" features an epigraph from Isaiah 13:21 in the *New Living Translation* of the Bible.

"Jeremiad" features an epigraph from Isaiah 5:8 in the *King James Version* of the Bible.

"*No ideas but in* objects" paraphrases William Carlos Williams in its title.

"The Future" references Miller Williams' poem "Animals" in its epigraph.

Acknowledgments

I am obliged to the editors of the following journals in which my poems appeared for the first time:

Barrelhouse: "The Human Animal";
Beloit Poetry Journal: "Stork";
The Cortland Review: "The Brass Bell";
The Greensboro Review: "Climate";
The Laurel Review: "The Two Near-Deaths of My Father Like the Resurrection of *Roseanne*";
The Massachusetts Review: "Algorithm";
Montreal International Poetry Prize Global Anthology: "As Soon as We Are Born We Start to Die";
Painted Bride Quarterly: "The Part of My Father Will Be Played by Jack Nicholson";
Pleiades: "Jeremiad";
Puerto del Sol: "Hiatus," "Sex and Violence," "My Father Tells the Story of Seeing Tanya Tucker Dancing on a Bar";
Radar Poetry: "Every Time You Type *Moth*, You Type *Mother*," "Environment," "Etymology of Gun," "*No ideas but in* objects," "Culling," "Vanitas";
Raritan: "The Year We Met";
The Southern Review: "Prophesy," "The 20 Gauge is Meant for Birds and Beginners";
swamp pink: "The Mirror of God Is Only Glass";
Your Impossible Voice: "How to Drive in Snow," "New Town."

Thank you to:

the North Carolina Arts Council for a 2019-2020 Fellowship;

the presses who listed individual poems as finalists for publication or prizes, especially the *Montreal International Poetry Prize Global Anthology* and *RADAR Poetry*;

BOA Editions, Ltd., especially Peter Conners, Justine Alfano, Benjamin Thompson, Isabella Madeira, Sandy Knight, Lydia Fanara, and Julia

White for including my book in this series and for all their help in editing, designing the cover, and sharing my manuscript;

Jennifer Whitaker and Jaimee Hills for their eyes and ears;

the dream poets John Gallaher and Chloe Honum;

and, finally, to Mavis, my dog, and Eb, my son, who fill me up with anxiety, love, and pride—and, my husband, David: there are no words.

About the Author

Jennie Malboeuf is the author of *jump the gun*, part of the American Poets Continuum Series (BOA Editions, 2025), and *God had a body*, awarded the 2019 Blue Light Books Prize by Adrian Matejka (Indiana UP, 2020). Her poems have appeared in *Pleiades*, *The Gettysburg Review*, *Virginia Quarterly Review*, *The Southern Review*, and *Harvard Review*. Born and raised in Kentucky, she received a BA at Centre College an MFA at the University of North Carolina at Greensboro, and is the recipient of a 2020 North Carolina Arts Council Fellowship. She lives in Kentucky with her husband, son, and dog.

BOA Editions, Ltd. American Poets Continuum Series

No. 1   *The Fuhrer Bunker: A Cycle of Poems in Progress*
        W. D. Snodgrass

No. 2   *She*
        M. L. Rosenthal

No. 3   *Living With Distance*
        Ralph J. Mills, Jr.

No. 4   *Not Just Any Death*
        Michael Waters

No. 5   *That Was Then: New and Selected Poems*
        Isabella Gardner

No. 6   *Things That Happen Where There Aren't Any People*
        William Stafford

No. 7   *The Bridge of Change: Poems 1974–1980*
        John Logan

No. 8   *Signatures*
        Joseph Stroud

No. 9   *People Live Here: Selected Poems 1949–1983*
        Louis Simpson

No. 10 *Yin*
        Carolyn Kizer

No. 11 *Duhamel: Ideas of Order in Little Canada*
        Bill Tremblay

No. 12 *Seeing It Was So*
        Anthony Piccione

No. 13 *Hyam Plutzik: The Collected Poems*

No. 14 *Good Woman: Poems and a Memoir 1969–1980*
        Lucille Clifton

No. 15 *Next: New Poems*
        Lucille Clifton

No. 16 *Roxa: Voices of the Culver Family*
        William B. Patrick

No. 17 *John Logan: The Collected Poems*

No. 18 *Isabella Gardner: The Collected Poems*

No. 19 *The Sunken Lightship*
        Peter Makuck

No. 20 *The City in Which I Love You*
        Li-Young Lee

No. 21 *Quilting: Poems 1987–1990*
        Lucille Clifton

No. 22 *John Logan: The Collected Fiction*

No. 23 *Shenandoah and Other Verse Plays*
        Delmore Schwartz

No. 24 *Nobody Lives on Arthur Godfrey Boulevard*
        Gerald Costanzo

No. 25 *The Book of Names: New and Selected Poems*
        Barton Sutter

No. 26 *Each in His Season*
        W. D. Snodgrass

No. 27	Wordworks: Poems Selected and New Richard Kostelanetz	No. 45	At My Ease: Uncollected Poems of the Fifties and Sixties David Ignatow
No. 28	What We Carry Dorianne Laux	No. 46	Trillium Richard Foerster
No. 29	Red Suitcase Naomi Shihab Nye	No. 47	Fuel Naomi Shihab Nye
No. 30	Song Brigit Pegeen Kelly	No. 48	Gratitude Sam Hamill
No. 31	The Fuehrer Bunker: The Complete Cycle W. D. Snodgrass	No. 49	Diana, Charles, & the Queen William Heyen
No. 32	For the Kingdom Anthony Piccione	No. 50	Plus Shipping Bob Hicok
No. 33	The Quicken Tree Bill Knott	No. 51	Cabato Sentora Ray Gonzalez
No. 34	These Upraised Hands William B. Patrick	No. 52	We Didn't Come Here for This William B. Patrick
No. 35	Crazy Horse in Stillness William Heyen	No. 53	The Vandals Alan Michael Parker
No. 36	Quick, Now, Always Mark Irwin	No. 54	To Get Here Wendy Mnookin
No. 37	I Have Tasted the Apple Mary Crow	No. 55	Living Is What I Wanted: Last Poems David Ignatow
No. 38	The Terrible Stories Lucille Clifton	No. 56	Dusty Angel Michael Blumenthal
No. 39	The Heat of Arrivals Ray Gonzalez	No. 57	The Tiger Iris Joan Swift
No. 40	Jimmy & Rita Kim Addonizio	No. 58	White City Mark Irwin
No. 41	Green Ash, Red Maple, Black Gum Michael Waters	No. 59	Laugh at the End of the World: Collected Comic Poems 1969–1999 Bill Knott
No. 42	Against Distance Peter Makuck	No. 60	Blessing the Boats: New and Selected Poems: 1988–2000 Lucille Clifton
No. 43	The Night Path Laurie Kutchins	No. 61	Tell Me Kim Addonizio
No. 44	Radiography Bruce Bond		

No. 62 *Smoke*
        Dorianne Laux
No. 63 *Parthenopi: New and Selected Poems*
        Michael Waters
No. 64 *Rancho Notorious*
        Richard Garcia
No. 65 *Jam*
        Joe-Anne McLaughlin
No. 66 *A. Poulin, Jr. Selected Poems*
        Edited, with an Introduction by Michael Waters
No. 67 *Small Gods of Grief*
        Laure-Anne Bosselaar
No. 68 *Book of My Nights*
        Li-Young Lee
No. 69 *Tulip Farms and Leper Colonies*
        Charles Harper Webb
No. 70 *Double Going*
        Richard Foerster
No. 71 *What He Took*
        Wendy Mnookin
No. 72 *The Hawk Temple at Tierra Grande*
        Ray Gonzalez
No. 73 *Mules of Love*
        Ellen Bass
No. 74 *The Guests at the Gate*
        Anthony Piccione
No. 75 *Dumb Luck*
        Sam Hamill
No. 76 *Love Song with Motor Vehicles*
        Alan Michael Parker
No. 77 *Life Watch*
        Willis Barnstone
No. 78 *The Owner of the House: New Collected Poems 1940–2001*
        Louis Simpson
No. 79 *Is*
        Wayne Dodd
No. 80 *Late*
        Cecilia Woloch
No. 81 *Precipitates*
        Debra Kang Dean
No. 82 *The Orchard*
        Brigit Pegeen Kelly
No. 83 *Bright Hunger*
        Mark Irwin
No. 84 *Desire Lines: New and Selected Poems*
        Lola Haskins
No. 85 *Curious Conduct*
        Jeanne Marie Beaumont
No. 86 *Mercy*
        Lucille Clifton
No. 87 *Model Homes*
        Wayne Koestenbaum
No. 88 *Farewell to the Starlight in Whiskey*
        Barton Sutter
No. 89 *Angels for the Burning*
        David Mura
No. 90 *The Rooster's Wife*
        Russell Edson
No. 91 *American Children*
        Jim Simmerman
No. 92 *Postcards from the Interior*
        Wyn Cooper
No. 93 *You & Yours*
        Naomi Shihab Nye
No. 94 *Consideration of the Guitar: New and Selected Poems 1986–2005*
        Ray Gonzalez
No. 95 *Off-Season in the Promised Land*
        Peter Makuck

No. 96	*The Hoopoe's Crown* Jacqueline Osherow	No. 114	*The Heaven-Sent Leaf* Katy Lederer
No. 97	*Not for Specialists:* *New and Selected Poems* W. D. Snodgrass	No. 115	*Struggling Times* Louis Simpson
No. 98	*Splendor* Steve Kronen	No. 116	*And* Michael Blumenthal
No. 99	*Woman Crossing a Field* Deena Linett	No. 117	*Carpathia* Cecilia Woloch
No. 100	*The Burning of Troy* Richard Foerster	No. 118	*Seasons of Lotus, Seasons of* *Bone* Matthew Shenoda
No. 101	*Darling Vulgarity* Michael Waters	No. 119	*Sharp Stars* Sharon Bryan
No. 102	*The Persistence of Objects* Richard Garcia	No. 120	*Cool Auditor* Ray Gonzalez
No. 103	*Slope of the Child Everlasting* Laurie Kutchins	No. 121	*Long Lens: New and Selected* *Poems* Peter Makuck
No. 104	*Broken Hallelujahs* Sean Thomas Dougherty	No. 122	*Chaos Is the New Calm* Wyn Cooper
No. 105	*Peeping Tom's Cabin:* *Comic Verse 1928–2008* X. J. Kennedy	No. 123	*Diwata* Barbara Jane Reyes
No. 106	*Disclamor* G.C. Waldrep	No. 124	*Burning of the Three Fires* Jeanne Marie Beaumont
No. 107	*Encouragement for a Man* *Falling to His Death* Christopher Kennedy	No. 125	*Sasha Sings the Laundry on the* *Line* Sean Thomas Dougherty
No. 108	*Sleeping with Houdini* Nin Andrews	No. 126	*Your Father on the Train of* *Ghosts* G.C. Waldrep and John Gallaher
No. 109	*Nomina* Karen Volkman	No. 127	*Ennui Prophet* Christopher Kennedy
No. 110	*The Fortieth Day* Kazim Ali	No. 128	*Transfer* Naomi Shihab Nye
No. 111	*Elephants & Butterflies* Alan Michael Parker	No. 129	*Gospel Night* Michael Waters
No. 112	*Voices* Lucille Clifton		
No. 113	*The Moon Makes Its Own Plea* Wendy Mnookin		

No. 130 *The Hands of Strangers: Poems from the Nursing Home*
  Janice N. Harrington
No. 131 *Kingdom Animalia*
  Aracelis Girmay
No. 132 *True Faith*
  Ira Sadoff
No. 133 *The Reindeer Camps and Other Poems*
  Barton Sutter
No. 134 *The Collected Poems of Lucille Clifton: 1965–2010*
No. 135 *To Keep Love Blurry*
  Craig Morgan Teicher
No. 136 *Theophobia*
  Bruce Beasley
No. 137 *Refuge*
  Adrie Kusserow
No. 138 *The Book of Goodbyes*
  Jillian Weise
No. 139 *Birth Marks*
  Jim Daniels
No. 140 *No Need of Sympathy*
  Fleda Brown
No. 141 *There's a Box in the Garage You Can Beat with a Stick*
  Michael Teig
No. 142 *The Keys to the Jail*
  Keetje Kuipers
No. 143 *All You Ask for Is Longing: New and Selected Poems 1994–2014*
  Sean Thomas Dougherty
No. 144 *Copia*
  Erika Meitner
No. 145 *The Chair: Prose Poems*
  Richard Garcia
No. 146 *In a Landscape*
  John Gallaher
No. 147 *Fanny Says*
  Nickole Brown
No. 148 *Why God Is a Woman*
  Nin Andrews
No. 149 *Testament*
  G.C. Waldrep
No. 150 *I'm No Longer Troubled by the Extravagance*
  Rick Bursky
No. 151 *Antidote for Night*
  Marsha de la O
No. 152 *Beautiful Wall*
  Ray Gonzalez
No. 153 *the black maria*
  Aracelis Girmay
No. 154 *Celestial Joyride*
  Michael Waters
No. 155 *Whereso*
  Karen Volkman
No. 156 *The Day's Last Light Reddens the Leaves of the Copper Beech*
  Stephen Dobyns
No. 157 *The End of Pink*
  Kathryn Nuernberger
No. 158 *Mandatory Evacuation*
  Peter Makuck
No. 159 *Primitive: The Art and Life of Horace H. Pippin*
  Janice N. Harrington
No. 160 *The Trembling Answers*
  Craig Morgan Teicher
No. 161 *Bye-Bye Land*
  Christian Barter
No. 162 *Sky Country*
  Christine Kitano
No. 163 *All Soul Parts Returned*
  Bruce Beasley
No. 164 *The Smoke of Horses*
  Charles Rafferty

No. 165 *The Second O of Sorrow*
         Sean Thomas Dougherty
No. 166 *Holy Moly Carry Me*
         Erika Meitner
No. 167 *Clues from the Animal Kingdom*
         Christopher Kennedy
No. 168 *Dresses from the Old Country*
         Laura Read
No. 169 *In Country*
         Hugh Martin
No. 170 *The Tiny Journalist*
         Naomi Shihab Nye
No. 171 *All Its Charms*
         Keetje Kuipers
No. 172 *Night Angler*
         Geffrey Davis
No. 173 *The Human Half*
         Deborah Brown
No. 174 *Cyborg Detective*
         Jillian Weise
No. 175 *On the Shores of Welcome Home*
         Bruce Weigl
No. 176 *Rue*
         Kathryn Nuernberger
No. 177 *Let's Become a Ghost Story*
         Rick Bursky
No. 178 *Year of the Dog*
         Deborah Paredez
No. 179 *Brand New Spacesuit*
         John Gallaher
No. 180 *How to Carry Water: Selected Poems of Lucille Clifton*
         Edited, with an Introduction by Aracelis Girmay
No. 181 *Caw*
         Michael Waters
No. 182 *Letters to a Young Brown Girl*
         Barbara Jane Reyes
No. 183 *Mother Country*
         Elana Bell
No. 184 *Welcome to Sonnetville, New Jersey*
         Craig Morgan Teicher
No. 185 *I Am Not Trying to Hide My Hungers from the World*
         Kendra DeColo
No. 186 *The Naomi Letters*
         Rachel Mennies
No. 187 *Tenderness*
         Derrick Austin
No. 188 *Ceive*
         B.K. Fischer
No. 189 *Diamonds*
         Camille Guthrie
No. 190 *A Cluster of Noisy Planets*
         Charles Rafferty
No. 191 *Useful Junk*
         Erika Meitner
No. 192 *Field Notes from the Flood Zone*
         Heather Sellers
No. 193 *A Season in Hell with Rimbaud*
         Dustin Pearson
No. 194 *Your Emergency Contact Has Experienced an Emergency*
         Chen Chen
No. 195 *A Tinderbox in Three Acts*
         Cynthia Dewi Oka
No. 196 *Little Mr. Prose Poem: Selected Poems of Russell Edson*
         Edited by Craig Morgan Teicher

No. 197 *The Dug-Up Gun Museum*
         Matt Donovan
No. 198 *Four in Hand*
         Alicia Mountain
No. 199 *Buffalo Girl*
         Jessica Q. Stark
No. 200 *Nomenclatures of Invisibility*
         Mahtem Shiferraw
No. 201 *Flare, Corona*
         Jeannine Hall Gailey
No. 202 *Death Prefers the Minor Keys*
         Sean Thomas Dougherty
No. 203 *Desire Museum*
         Danielle Deulen
No. 204 *Transitory*
         Subhaga Crystal Bacon
No. 205 *Every Hard Sweetness*
         Sheila Carter-Jones
No. 206 *Blue on a Blue Palette*
         Lynne Thompson
No. 207 *One Wild Word Away*
         Geffrey Davis
No. 208 *The Strange God Who Makes Us*
         Christopher Kennedy
No. 209 *Our Splendid Failure to Do the Impossible*
         Rebecca Lindenberg
No. 210 *Yard Show*
         Janice N. Harrington
No. 211 *The Last Song of the World*
         Joseph Fasano
No. 212 *Lonely Women Make Good Lovers*
         Keetje Kuipers
No. 213 *jump the gun*
         Jennie Malboeuf

Colophon

BOA Editions, Ltd., a not-for-profit publisher of
poetry and other literary works, fosters readership and appreciation
of contemporary literature. By identifying, cultivating, and publishing
both new and established poets and selecting authors of unique literary
talent, BOA brings high-quality literature to the public.

Support for this effort comes from the sale of its publications,
grant funding, and private donations.

*

*The publication of this book is made possible, in part,
by the special support of the following individuals:*

Anonymous (x2)
Angela Bonazinga & Catherine Lewis
Ralph Black & Susan Murphy
Chris Dahl, *in honor of Chuck Hertrick*
Jonathan Everitt
David Fraher, *in memory of A. Poulin Jr.*
Bonnie Garner
James Hale
Peg Heminway
Charlotte & Raul Herrera
Nora A. Jones
Joe & Dale Klein
Barbara Lovenheim, *in memory of John Lovenheim*
Joe McElveney
Daniel M. Meyers, *in honor of J. Shepard Skiff*
Boo Poulin, *in memory of A. Poulin Jr.*
Deborah Ronnen
John H. Schultz
William Waddell & Linda Rubel
Michael Waters & Mihaela Moscaliuc

www.ingramcontent.com/pod-product-compliance
Lightning Source LLC
Chambersburg PA
CBHW031437230425
25484CB00002BA/4